HOW TO SURVIVE COLLEGE

Published by Scholastic India Pvt. Ltd.
A subsidiary of Scholastic Inc., New York, 10012 (USA).
Publishers since 1920, with international operations in Canada, Australia, New Zealand, the United Kingdom, India, and Hong Kong.

For information regarding permission, write to:
Scholastic India Pvt. Ltd.
A-27, Ground Floor, Sigma Centre
Infocity-1, Sector 34, Gurgaon-122001 (India)

First edition: August 2020

ISBN-13: 978-93-9018-907-6

Printed in India at Sai Printo Pack Pvt Ltd, New Delhi.

HOW TO SURVIVE COLLEGE

SIMRAN TAPADIA

SCHOLASTIC
New York Toronto London Auckland
Sydney New Delhi Hong Kong

A MESSAGE FROM SCHOLASTIC INDIA

The transition from school to college can be a tricky one, but also tons of fun. I still remember my college days!

This book is unlike anything we've ever published. Gorgeously designed, it navigates the reader through the trials and tribulations, loves and heartbreaks, and everything in between that comes with college life.

I'd recommend it to anyone who is going to enter college, is in college or anyone who wants to reminisce.

Shantanu Duttagupta
Publisher

To my family and better half for believing in me.

CONTENTS

COLLEGE

ROOM-MATES

RELATIONSHIPS

THE WORKING LIFE

College

THINGS TO KNOW BEFORE GETTING INTO COLLEGE

RIGHT STREAM Choosing the right stream can be confusing for some, especially with the variety of courses on offer nowadays. You need to know where your passion lies and whether you are ready to pursue it with the same enthusiasm every day. Too many options can get overwhelming, so it's a good idea to ask someone experienced for advice.

LOCATION Where would you prefer your college to be located? For example, I had gotten into two institutes: One was in the heart of the city and the other was outside town, surrounded by nature. I chose the one outside town because I prefer nature's peace and quiet over the commotion of the city. Another factor that matters is whether you want to live at home, or you want to move out. Accordingly, you need to prioritize your hunt for the right college.

ATMOSPHERE What kind of peer group are you looking for in your college? Competitive? Niche? Relaxed? Every college has a different kind of crowd. Your college should suit your personality, since the atmosphere of the school will impact you as an individual. So you should try to visit the school before applying and speak to the alumni or the present students.

MONEY College isn't cheap. You can opt for scholarships or student loans. You can freelance or take up any part-time job to pay your bills and miscellaneous expenditure. Try to look for internships to get some work experience during your semester breaks.

NO SLEEP Well, no doubt college is fun and exciting, but there will be days when you'll feel exhausted. Expect some long sleepless nights. Just working in class won't suffice; you'll need to stay up late to work on your projects. You might also need to redo the work to make it more thought-provoking and engaging.

NO BACKGROUND It's not compulsory to have a background in what you are about to pursue; just follow your passion and be true to yourself. Your parents don't need to be from that field. If they are, that's great. But it is your passion that will drive you and take you places.

LOTS OF TALKING You'll be required to do a lot of talking while presenting your ideas. Be clear and confident while explaining them. You should also know how to take criticism. During one of my reviews, my faculty was rude enough to make me cry. But that made me look at my work from a different perspective. Be strong.

'I WANT TO GIVE UP' There will be moments, days or weeks when you'll feel like giving up. You might compare yourself to others. It's OK; it's all a part of learning. Take this as an opportunity to learn from your peers and be motivated by them, because it is easy to feel demotivated. Since I was an art student, there were times the art I worked on for hours would end up in the trash. But that's OK. You just have to move forward and practice more, and never forget why you started.

HOW TO ADJUST TO A NEW CITY

EXPLORE

A fun way to explore the city is through food walks and history walks. This way you get to meet new people in the group and make new friends. If you choose to go out alone, do keep your safety in mind and keep someone updated about your whereabouts.

FIND WHAT YOU LOVE

Get yourself a new hobby. Join a dance class or a nature club, or learn a new sport or skill. This is a good way to socialize and meet new people.

KEEP IN TOUCH

Keep in touch with your friends and family back home. It will help you feel less lonely. Technology today has made communication and keeping in touch so much easier. However, you will have to make the effort to maintain your relationships.

PATIENCE

You'll need to keep calm if you are unable fall in love with a new place right away. You'll have to adjust and try to find things you like about it.

TYPES OF PEOPLE IN COLLEGE

We meet various kinds of people in our lifetime, but the most memorable ones are those we meet in college. We encounter the best and the worst, and they all help us understand others and ourselves.

THE COOL ONE

- Liked by all.
- Funny.
- Good-looking.

THE LOUD ONE

- Talks nonsense.
- Loves attention.
- Annoying.

THE WANNABE

- Wants to be popular.
- Wants to be accepted.
- Copies the popular kids.

THE CREEPSTER

- Creeps around you.
- Stares a lot.
- Stalks you on social media.

THE HIPPIE

- Opens their mouth just to say, 'Wanna smoke?'

THE SILENT BOMB

- Doesn't talk much.
- Minds his/her business.
- Mysterious.

THE FLIRT

- Makes everyone feel special.
- Sweet-talker.
- Isn't serious.

THE ATHLETE

- Loves sports.
- Talks as if he/she is sponsoring a sports team.

THE GYM FREAK

- Talks about protein shakes.
- Gives tips on exercising.
- Gym is their first home.

THE NICE HOOMAN

- You want to be BFFs with them.
- Is there for you in your time of need and liked by all.

THE NERD

- Cute and annoying.
- Love comics and books.
- Really smart.

THE OLD SOUL

- Advice-giver.
- Problem-solver.
- Secret-keeper.

THE STINKER
- Stinks of something foul.
- You can't sit or even stand beside them.

THE DIRTY-TALKER
- Makes every conversation dirty.
- 'That's what she/he said' is their tag line.

THE FOREVER-SINGLE
- Tries really hard to get a partner.
- Gets rejected all the time.

THE PARTY ANIMAL
- Never sober.
- Has more knowledge about clubs than class.
- Shows off on social media.

THE GAMER
- Gaming is life.
- Has a better virtual life than a real one.

THE WINGMAN
- Introduces you to suitable partners.
- Takes care of you when you are rejected.

THE LOVER

- Falls in love with someone new every day.

THE TEACHER'S PET

- Answers every question.
- Always found lurking near the staff room and is a suck-up.

THE LAZY BUM

- Never attends class.
- Loves sleeping.
- Too lazy to go out or do anything.

THE 'I'M BROKE!'

- Never has money.
- Always borrowing money.

THE MOM

- Knows what is where.
- Has all the supplies handy.
- Caring and warm.

THE OVER-INVOLVED

- Participates and volunteers for every event.
- Knows half the campus.

THE CLINGER

- Always texts you.
- Always wants to hangout.
- Never leaves your sight.

THE KNOW-IT-ALL

- Thinks they are the most intelligent student.
- Loves proving others wrong.
- Oversmart and irritating.

THE SELFIE ADDICT

- Too much attitude.
- Pretentious.
- Self-obsessed.

THE WORKAHOLIC

- Smart and knowledgeable.
- Has a great work ethic.
- Inspires others.

THE ONE IN A LDR

- Respects their partner.
- Loyal.
- Has patience.

THE HOT ONE

- Smells good and looks good.
- Great dresser.
- Everybody stops and stares.

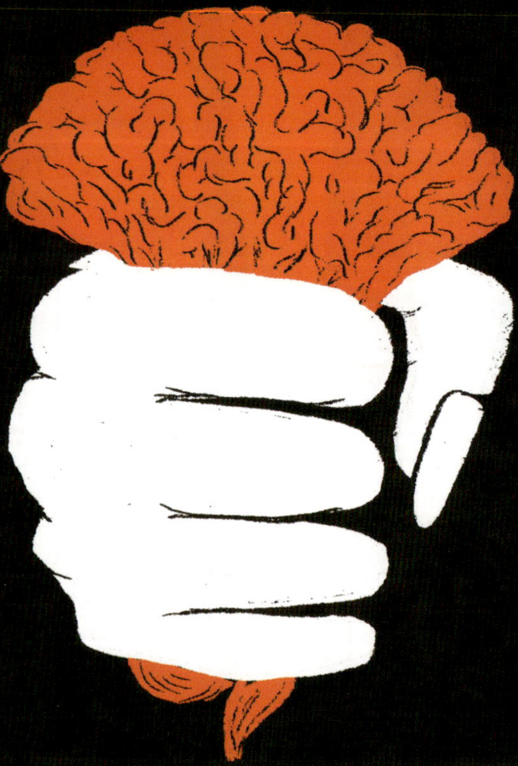

STRESS MANAGEMENT

College life can get stressful and difficult to manage. We all could practice a few habits to reduce our stress.

BREATHE

Sometimes things can be overwhelming and stressful. It may seem like many things are happening all at once. Don't freak out. It's easy to lash out at people around us, so take a step back and look at the situation calmly and objectively. This will help you learn how to multitask on a hundred projects at once.

MAKE A LIST

Prioritize and work accordingly. Making a list helps you understand what you should finish first. It clears your mind; that way you have less stress keeping a tab on everything that you have to do, making your life a little easier.

FOOD

For a healthy mind, eat healthy. Don't just survive on junk food. Being away from home adds to the pressure to eat junk. But if you stay at home, you should take advantage of home-cooked food. Fresh food has nutrients that the body needs and which impact your creativity in ways you might not realize. Lastly, do not forget to drink lots and lots of water. Keep that rocking body of yours hydrated all the time.

SLEEP

By adding sleep here, I know I'm contradicting what I said earlier in 'Things to know before getting into college', but you need the right amount of rest as well. You aren't a machine. Lack of sleep affects productivity and creativity. For me, when I don't sleep well, I'm unable to think of new ideas or create something new. Besides, you don't want to graduate with dark circles and a sunken face.

LEARN TO SAY 'NO'

Don't be a people-pleaser. At the start of college, I tried to fit into places where I didn't belong. Just because you want people to like you doesn't mean you have to say 'yes' to everything. It's OK to say 'NO'. The moment you realize that not everyone is going to like you, your life will change for the better. You can't change everyone's perspective about you because at the end of the day you have to be true to yourself.

TALK IT OUT

Talking to someone reduces your stress by half. You can also seek the help of a counsellor, if needed. Every college usually has a counsellor who is there to listen to you and help you.

NO SUBSTANCES

Indulging in alcohol or other substances to take the pressure off your day is not the right approach. Once you start down this path, it becomes easier to find more and more reasons to get hooked. It then becomes a way for you to escape reality, which is harmful in the long run.

HOW TO DEAL WITH 'TEACHERS'

Sometimes there are teachers who can be tough to deal with. They may be hard on you or you may believe they treat you unfairly. Whatever the cause, here are some things you can do to help fix the rift.

1 SHUT UP

No one likes a disruptor in the classroom. Don't be the one who creates commotion and disturbance. It ruins the mood and the flow of the teacher—all the more reason for them to not like you. Talk once the lecture is over. Or just pass a chit.

2 IGNORE

The teacher of one of my interior design classes did not like me. She would often yell at me in class. It can be insulting but it's OK. You don't have to see the teacher's face every day, just for a few hours every week. So, learn to ignore these things.

3 RESPECT

Respect your teacher, no matter what. They are your guru, and there will always be something valuable that they will teach you. You must not get disheartened just because they aren't treating you right. You must stick to your morals and ethics and carry on. And don't be late to class.

4 PARTICIPATE

Participation shows enthusiasm. But try to talk sense. Many students like talking rubbish just to get the teacher's attention, which is more annoying. I knew a bunch of such people who would constantly interrupt the teacher and disturb the class.

5 COMMUNICATE

If the teacher's behaviour is bothering you, talk to them and address the situation. Tell them how their behaviour is affecting you. Perhaps they aren't doing it intentionally. Talking things out helps.

6 STEP INTO THEIR SHOES

When you realize that a teacher doesn't like you, you should ask yourself why. Look at the situation from their perspective: Maybe it is your behaviour or something that you did intentionally or unintentionally which might have hurt them. We all are humans and we all make mistakes.

7 PAY ATTENTION

Paying attention in class is important; no one likes a student who is distracted. It's quite disrespectful when you aren't paying attention to your teacher. You don't need to show them that you think their lecture is boring.

TIME MANAGEMENT

CHECKLIST IS YOUR BFF

A checklist is like a daily goal or a bucket list for the day. Making one helps to stay on track and get work done faster and efficiently. If you prefer using technology to organize yourself, there are many apps and tools to help you keep track of all your projects. The tasks need not be just your college work; there can be deadlines to pay rent, grocery shopping and other miscellaneous stuff. For me, my checklist is like a game. I'm always excited to tick off a finished task.

EXERCISE TO RELAX

Our body is a temple and we need to worship it. Taking out thirty minutes for your body every day to exercise or even go for walk always helps. It is beneficial to keep your body working well.

NO DISTRACTION

It can get overwhelming when you have a lot on your plate, which can tempt you to procrastinate and get distracted. However, the more you delay your work, the more it will pile up. Technology too has become a huge distraction for us. We end up spending hours on social media only to regret it later. Choose your distractions wisely.

VII

'YOU WILL NEVER "FIND" TIME FOR ANYTHING. IF YOU WANT TIME, YOU MUST MAKE IT.'

CHARLES BUXTON

I

Time management is essential for a productive and organized life. It helps you stay grounded and on track.

PRIORITIZE

II

Mark all your submissions on the calendar to make sure which one to prioritize first. A Saturday night party shouldn't be your priority when you have a lot of work pending. What I mean is, you need to be smart while choosing your priorities. Some days you'll even need to prioritize yourself first because at the end of the day, you need to take care of yourself as well.

STAY ORGANIZED

III

Organizing your things helps you have a clear idea of where things are. Time management isn't just about managing time but also about managing your things. Staying organized helps you reduce stress and anxiety, and work efficiently.

FIND THE RIGHT BALANCE

IV

We need to find a balance between everything that's happening around us so that it doesn't get overwhelming. It is important to balance the various elements in your life like sleeping, eating, exercising and working, along with giving yourself a little me time as well.

V

DEADLINES

1 SET DEADLINES

It's helpful to set deadlines for yourself before the actual deadline. That way if there is any issue, you have enough time to solve or work on it before the actual deadline. They help you become responsible and increase your speed, efficiency and your ability to deal with multiple projects at once.

2 BREAK IT DOWN

If you're working on a huge project, you can break it down and work on it part by part. That way you get to understand the project in greater depth, making your work detailed and comprehensive.

3 DON'T OVER-COMMIT

When you're working on a deadline, don't commit yourself to other new work. This will only add to your stress. Better to keep your workload limited and focus on what you have on your plate.

College life can feel like a roller-coaster ride, but with proper deadlines and priorities you can enjoy this ride with all it's ups and downs.

4 DON'T WAIT

There is no such thing as waiting for inspiration. Don't give yourself excuses saying, 'Hey, I'm waiting for a spark of creativity.' Get inspired by reading books, meeting your peers, talking to your mentors and and looking at the works of other artists. Inspiration can strike at any time, so it's best to keep yourself going.

5 REWARD YOURSELF

Rewarding yourself when you meet your deadline is a wonderful way to stay motivated. It has a great positive impact on the brain since you know that if you finish a particular task, you'll get rewarded. And of course, who doesn't like gifts!

6 START!

You should start thinking about your project as soon as you get it. Keep your mind running to come up with new ideas. Start thinking in that direction and take note of things that might help you with the project.

PUBLIC SPEAKING

Public speaking can be scary and heart-wrenching, and in college you will have to give speeches whether you like it or not. The following tips will help you get over this fear and face the task with confidence.

GET INSPIRED BY THE PROS

Read up about Martin Luther King Jr., Oprah, Barack Obama, Greta Thunberg or whoever inspires you. Such leaders can teach you to be confident and articulate, to hold the audience's attention and to put your thoughts across in a cohesive manner.

SMILE

Look happy while talking to your audience, because no one likes a grumpy person. Of course, don't smile too much as that will look creepy. A smile is always warm and welcoming to anyone you talk to. A smile says a lot about a person.

BE COMFORTABLE

To make others feel comfortable, you need to be comfortable yourself. The way you talk, move your hands and walk shows your comfort level. Try not to fidget while talking.

KNOW YOUR AUDIENCE

Understand who you are presenting your work to and prepare accordingly. If you are required to address your faculty, you should talk formally; be informal while addressing your classmates.

THE PURPOSE OF YOUR SPEECH

You should be able to convey your message clearly. If your thoughts are not clear, it will be difficult to keep your audience's attention. You can't expect to move people without knowing your content.

BE LOUD

Practice your pitch. It's beneficial to be loud enough to address the very last person in the room. But don't be too loud, or you'll scare them off.

DON'T APOLOGIZE

Don't apologize for the mistakes you make while talking. Others might not notice them at all, so it's OK. Just be confident. Put on that big beautiful smile of yours, get on that stage and rock it. Because you're going to ace that speech.

FAKE IT TILL YOU MAKE IT

Public speaking is an art and not everyone is born with it. However, one can always learn and improve. You may not be confident but your audience doesn't need to know that. Your body language will speak a lot about you, so even pretending to be confident will work.

Like it or not, you'll end up having an all-nighter sometimes. You'll go to class with a dull face and puffy eyes. But by the end of college, you will have a heart filled with memories of being up with your friends, fooling around and talking nonsense. For now, to overcome the effects of an all-nighter, here's what might help.

PUFFY EYES

The easiest way to tell if a person is sleep-deprived is by their eyes. Our eyes tend to get puffy and develop dark circles due to a lack of sleep. To get rid of them, you could use a cold compress over your eyes for ten to fifteen minutes. You can also use a concealer for the dark circles. If you get red eyes, you can use a warm compress to shrink the blood vessels in the eye. Drinking lots of water also helps in reducing puffiness and dark circles.

TAKE A SHOWER

If you've pulled an all-nighter, there is a high chance that you will skip your bath. But you need to drag yourself to the bathroom and get under that shower. This will help wake your body and make you feel fresh and alive. When your body doesn't get enough sleep, the skin can become dry and puffy. Scrubbing and bathing not only increases blood flow but also makes you look less pale. And once you get out of that nice and refreshing shower, you'll feel less dead and more alive, and you'll look good as well.

SELF-CARE

No matter what your reason for pulling an all-nighter is, you need to understand that this will affect your body in the long run. You'll age faster and have wrinkles due to pale and dull skin. The concept of beauty sleep isn't just a myth. Sleep helps to rejuvenate your skin. It allows your body to refuel and helps you feel good inside and out.

HOW TO LOOK FRESH AFTER A SLEEPLESS NIGHT

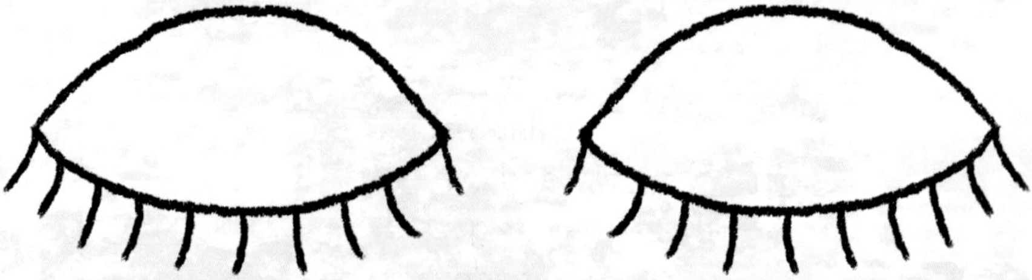

HOW TO STAY AWAKE IN CLASS

We all struggle to stay awake in class no matter the time of the day, even though it's really beneficial if we do actually pay attention. If you find it difficult to stay awake, here are a few things that have helped me keep my eyes open.

SIT IN THE MIDDLE

Sitting at the back or at the front will definitely bring attention to you. The best place to hide your drowsy face is in the middle of the classroom. You'll merge with your classmates and your faculty won't notice that you are yawning in their classes.

POWER ALARM

You can set alarms on your phone that are fifteen minutes apart. Keep your phone on vibrate so you don't disturb the class.

CAFFEINE KICK

Caffeine is a psychostimulant that increases wakefulness, attentiveness, the ability to focus and overall energy levels. Caffeine isn't a particularly healthy choice but does get the work done for a little while. Just don't get addicted to it.

KEEP EATING

Keep a box of munchies at hand. Food provides energy which helps you stay active and attentive. Of course, don't get crispy food and distract the class. My teacher caught me eating one time, so I told him that I would faint if I didn't eat. After that, he always allowed me to eat during his lectures.

TEAM-WORK

Ask your desk neighbour to poke you in case you fall asleep and vice versa. That way both of you will stay awake.

GET ENOUGH SLEEP

This will be difficult to achieve for as long as the Internet exists. While distractions are hard to get rid of, try to manage your time well so that you get enough sleep. Make sleep your bae and you'll not regret it.

TRICK 'EM

Get eyes printed and paste them on your spectacles. Then you can put them on and easily pass out in class. Just make sure you don't snore. LOL, I'm obviously kidding.

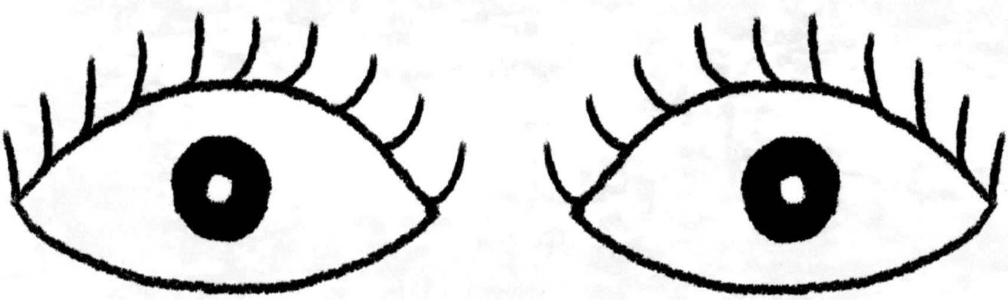

EXAMS!

Sleep well
58008
EXAMS!!!
22:00
I can do this...
But how should
I do this?

One usually equates the word 'exam' with stress. Here are a few things we can do to ease the pressure.

MAKE NOTES

Sometimes making complete notes can get difficult. A pro tip to deal with this is writing down pointers or keywords. Besides, when you have a lot to study, it's easier to just go through the points when revising. Mugging up is not a good idea. It's better to understand the topic. Not only will you remember it better, you will also learn from it.

TEACH YOUR FRIENDS

Teaching your friends is a really great way to remember and revise what you have studied. It helps you recall everything and if you can explain it to someone else, you can definitely write about it in the paper.

DRINK WATER

Keep yourself hydrated. Drink a good amount of water while you study so that your brain retains new information faster. But don't end up drinking so much that you spend half your time in the bathroom.

TREAT YOUR TUMMY

During lengthy study sessions, when you'll feel like you deserve a treat, or perhaps you don't have time to cook, junk food can be super-tempting. But what you eat has an impact on your energy levels and focus, so stay away from junk. Choose food that is nutritious and less acidic so you don't mess up your tummy.

SLEEP

Get enough sleep before the test. Sleep is a way to rest your brain. It will help you recover information faster and better. It will also keep you away from distractions and unnecessary drama.

RELAX

Don't stress about your exam as it won't do you any good. Take deep breaths and be confident about what you have studied. Of course, if you haven't prepared, then only your luck can save you. Don't cheat.

LIFE OUTSIDE THE CLASSROOM

College life is usually full and busy. There are courses to take, careers to decide, lots of new ideas to think about and friends to make. You will get so busy with finishing college that you might forget that there's more to this life than lectures and studying. A holistic college experience is what you should aim for.

Here are a few experiences I had and cherish the most. You can write down what you would like to do and add to the list below.

- ☐ LIVE WITH A ROOM-MATE.
- ☐ PULL AN ALL-NIGHTER.
- ☐ TAKE ADVANTAGE OF YOUR STUDENT-ID DISCOUNT.
- ☐ PARTICIPATE IN A COLLEGE EVENT.
- ☐ SIT IN A RANDOM CLASS WHICH ISN'T YOUR MAJOR.
- ☐ LEARN TO COOK A MEAL.
- ☐ CREATE A JOURNAL.
- ☐ APPRECIATE THE TEACHER WHO MEANT SOMETHING TO YOU.
- ☐ TAKE A VIDEO OF YOU WALKING TO YOUR CLASS.
- ☐ TELL YOUR CRUSH YOU LIKE THEM.
- ☐ STAND UP FOR YOURSELF AND SOMEONE ELSE.
- ☐ FALL IN LOVE.
- ☐ DO AN INTERNSHIP.
- ☐ BE PROUD OF YOURSELF.
- ☐ ____________________
- ☐ ____________________
- ☐ ____________________
- ☐ ____________________
- ☐ ____________________
- ☐ ____________________
- ☐ ____________________
- ☐ ____________________
- ☐ ____________________
- ☐ ____________________

BUDDY BUCKET LIST

College life is synonymous with great friendships, which are often lifelong. From late-night chats which end at daybreak, sneaking food into class and sharing it under the table and playing silly pranks on each other, there are lots of experiences we share with our buddies.

I have jotted down a few things I did. Now you can add to the list with what you wish to do with your buddies before graduation.

- ☐ Take a road trip.
- ☐ Take lots of videos and photos of your friends.
- ☐ Prank your friends.
- ☐ ____________________
- ☐ ____________________
- ☐ ____________________
- ☐ ____________________
- ☐ ____________________
- ☐ ____________________
- ☐ ____________________
- ☐ ____________________
- ☐ ____________________
- ☐ ____________________
- ☐ ____________________
- ☐ ____________________
- ☐ ____________________
- ☐ ____________________
- ☐ ____________________

SELF-CARE

Taking care of yourself is as important as breathing. One can't live with poor mental health. Taking some time out for yourself from your busy schedule is healthy. Here are a few things that helped me. You can try them too.

SLEEP

Sleep helps calm your nerves and have a fresh mind once you wake up. But don't use sleep as an escape from your reality.

FOOD

Your body is your temple. So try not to throw garbage in your temple. Healthy food is essential for a healthy mind and soul.

BE KIND TO YOURSELF

Don't be too hard on yourself. Don't give in to self-loathing. Talking negatively to yourself comes easier than talking positively. Go easy on yourself. At the end of the day, you have to live with yourself and love yourself more than anyone else.

TRAVEL

I know it's easy to say 'Go travel'. But travel need not mean going out of town. You can simply take a day off and explore the city you live in. It's refreshing and will energize your mind.

BE HAPPY

You should do what makes you happy and calms your nerves. We all have different ideas of self-care. Just make sure you treat your mind and soul well. You can also go for therapy if that helps.
At the end of the day, we all want someone to listen to us.

Cloud 9

Apart from studies and a new culture, you will also be exposed to other things. You'll be tempted to experiment. It's our choice whether we want to indulge in it or not. Here are a few dos and don'ts to keep in mind.

PEER PRESSURE

No one can force you! There will be people around you who will try to force you or pressurize you into doing things you won't approve of. Consider those people as RED FLAGS and distance yourself from them. You don't need to conform to their idea of fun and get into situations you aren't comfortable with.

TALK IT OUT

If you're feeling anxious, you should talk to someone about it. Tell a friend you trust what you are feeling. I went through a similar situation where people around me were into such activities and I started feeling left out. So I spoke to my elder brother about it and he discussed it with me and made me realize what's best for me. Talking to someone you trust is always advisable.

BE CONFIDENT

You don't need to feel insecure or think less of yourself if you aren't 'one of those kids'. It's not something to feel proud of anyway. You should be confident in your own skin and know what's best for you. At the end of the day, you need to take care of yourself.

IN CASE

If you do wish to try it out, do remember a few things. Do it with people you trust and feel comfortable with. It's all right if you don't like it. You can stop and walk away from there.

ROOM-MATES
TYPES OF ROOM-MATES
HOW TO ADJUST TO YOUR ROOM-MATE
WHAT TO DO IF YOU AND YOUR ROOM-MATE DON'T GET ALONG

TYPES OF

THE CLEAN FREAK
They'll clean your things since they don't like a messy room. They are obsessed with cleaning which can also get on your nerves.

THE SLOB
They are messy and dirty, and don't pick up their stuff. They have their things lying around for ages, especially dirty dishes, which end up stinking.

THE GHOST
You hardly see them at home. They come and go, but you won't notice. They are the best because you get the whole room to yourself.

THE PARTY ANIMAL
They won't let you live in peace. They may drag you to a party and force booze down your throat too. Just make your boundaries clear.

THE HERMIT
They are in the room 24/7. They don't attend classes. How they pass is a mystery. They may not interfere in your life.

THE OBSESSED ONE
They want to be best friends forever. They are obsessed with you and want to do everything together. They also ask too many questions.

THE THIEF
They don't understand the difference between borrowing and stealing. They take your things without permission, and even use them in front of you, pretending that it's theirs.

THE BORROWER
They borrow your things and never return them, except in some cases. But only if you're lucky enough to find such a room-mate.

ROOMIES

THE OWNER

They behave like they own the house. They make their own rules and expect you to follow them. They are quite annoying.

THE 'THIRD' ROOM-MATE

If your room-mate is in a relationship, they might bring their partners over. They are like an uninvited guest, so bye-bye to privacy.

THE HIGH ROOMIE

They are always stoned and the room reeks. They are slow and won't bother you much. But your only issue will be hygiene and *THE SMELL*.

THE FOOD THIEF

This one will always steal your food even though you tell them not to. Eventually, you'll start hiding your food.

THE PASSIVE-AGGRESSIVE ONE

They will talk to you sweetly about things that bother them. But if you request them for anything, they'll have an issue about it.

THE LOVE MACHINE

They are obnoxiously loud. It gets really uncomfortable being in the room as you can always hear their lovey-dovey phone calls with their partner.

THE MOODY ONE

They are unpredictable. You never know what their mood will be like, so you walk on eggshells around them.

THE PERFECT ROOMIE

The perfect room-mate doesn't exist. Nah, I'm kidding, they do. They know their boundaries, and are clean, nice and fun to be with.

How to adjust to your room-mate

Since most of us have grown up living in our own comfort zone, it gets a tad bit uncomfortable to share our personal space with a stranger. So here are a few things you could do to adjust.

SET HOUSE RULES
It's good to lay down some ground rules of dos and don'ts. If you don't like noise or the light on while you sleep, for instance, just say so.

RESOLVE PROBLEMS ASAP
Communication is the key to a healthy relationship. If there's an issue, it's better to talk and clear things up. If they ate your food, tell them that you didn't like it and not to repeat it in the future.

ASK BEFORE INVITING
It's good to inform your room-mate before inviting someone over. It's their room too and no one likes uninvited guests.

THEIR STUFF IS THEIRS
Understand the value of each other belongings. Make sure to not use anything without each other's permission and even if you are using them, do so with care.

LOCK THE HOUSE

Make sure you lock the house before leaving as you don't want intruders. Remember, you aren't the only one living in the house; you are sharing it with someone else.

BE OPEN-MINDED

They might have different habits and a different upbringing from yours. You need to have an open mind about the things your room-mates do and adjust accordingly.

YOU MAY NOT BECOME LIFELONG FRIENDS

Not everyone gets lucky with room-mates who turn into lifelong friends. You need to understand that not everyone you meet will stay in your life forever.

BE NEAT

No one likes a messy room-mate. An untidy place creates turmoil and disturbance within which one might not even realize. A neat room will uplift your mood.

PRIVACY

One should always respect each other's personal space. You need to understand and give each other privacy. For instance, try not to use each other's things without permission.

RESPECT

It doesn't matter where you come from. It's important to treat each other with respect. The way you treat someone else says a lot about you.

What
TO DO IF
YOU AND
YOUR ROOM-MATE
don't
get
along

FIGURE OUT THE PROBLEM

It's usually a good idea to talk things out. A conversation can help you understand the reasons for the conflict and clear assumptions; you might even come up with a solution. No one likes to come to a house that has negative energy. It's better to go to bed in a happy home than a sad one.

DISTANCE YOURSELF

If talking things out doesn't help, try to not cross each other's path. Make sure you don't do anything to offend or disrespect them regardless of how they treat you. It's OK if you don't get along but you don't need to show it. Since you are living together under the same roof, it is better to maintain peace, keep your distance and be positive.

FIND A MIDDLE GROUND

If you and your room-mate don't get along, try to reach to a middle ground. Divide up your space as equally as possible and set boundaries. Make a list of rules and chores that both of you agree on and will follow. For example, the top shelf of the fridge can be your room-mate's and the bottom can be yours. This way, both of you get your own space and neither of you are invading the other's.

REVENGE IS A FOOL'S GAME

No matter how bad your room-mate is, you have no right to take revenge. There is no point in putting your energy into someone who isn't worth your time. You can either try moving out or find another room-mate. Sometimes that won't be possible, so you will have to come up with a solution to deal with them or learn to ignore them. We all have better things to do in our lives than be petty.

RELATIONSHIPS

How to know if someone likes you

Having someone like you is a very special feeling. You might not end up reciprocating the same feelings, but it sure does make you feel good. Here are a few things I had experienced when someone had a crush on me.

1 TALK

Not everyone is interested in what you ate for dinner last night. Only two people will ask you this: one is your mother (Haha!) and the other is someone who's trying to get your attention. The latter will genuinely show great interest in your life, the things you do; even simple silly things will interest them.

2 SOCIAL MEDIA

Even after classes, they'll stay in touch via text or call or through social media. If they send you a post on a topic you guys spoke about earlier, you know you've been on their minds.

3 **'LET'S HANG OUT'**

Well, if someone asks you to hang out after college hours, it doesn't necessarily mean that they have a thing for you. It depends on what they plan to do and if they're inviting other people too.

4 **CONVERSATION-KEEPER**

Sometimes, while talking to someone new, it may happen that the conversation dies and we don't know what to talk about next. But if this person is interested in you, he/she will make the effort to keep the conversation going and ask to share experiences with them.

5 **THEY FAVOUR YOU**

If you are in an argument, they will always side with you. If someone is talking trash about you, they will support you. It is their way of showing that they are sweet on you. If there's a group assignment, they will prefer to work with you.

6 **'MAY I SIT HERE?'**

Not everyone will risk talking while the teacher is in the class. They'll initiate conversation while you study and crack jokes to make you laugh.

> **'My advice would be to not lead someone on if you know that they have a crush on you but you're not interested in them. It's best to let them know politely. I have seen many people leading people on just for the thrill of the attention they get. They don't understand that the other person has feelings as well and it is going to break their heart if you toy with them.'**

At some point in our lives, all of us develop a crush. So if you have feelings for someone, you should let them know; cause if you don't someone else will. It's OK to take the first step and put yourself out there.

SHOW YOUR INTEREST

For someone to know that you are interested, you have to show them, because they aren't gonna get a dream that you have a crush on them. Give them attention, tell them that they look good or appreciate their work. Don't get too clingy though.

SMILE

If you have a crush on them, the best way to make them notice you is through a smile. Don't make it creepy. Don't make it too obvious that you were looking at them. But please don't stare and look away.

STALKING RULES

It's a common tendency to check their social media out if you have a crush. Don't start liking all their pictures. That's just outrageously creepy. No one wants to wake up with notifications of you liking their pictures from back in 2008 or 2009. It's all right to go down memory lane but don't make it too obvious that you were looking them up.

BE CONFIDENT

No matter what, always be confident. For instance, if your crush catches you looking at them, be confident enough to either walk it off or look them in the eye and smile. One needs to be confident about themselves in order to handle any situation. Everyone loves a confident person but not an overconfident person; they just come out as arrogant.

What to do when you have a crush on someone

TRY TALKING

If you haven't really spoken to them then you should initiate a conversation. Often, you only focus on their pretty face, and as soon as they open their mouth, your feelings for them come crashing down; perhaps their perspective on something is off. That's why some people are better off as a crush. The best thing you can do is actually talk to them to see who they really are. There are chances that you might not like them after all.

DON'T OVERTHINK

This is a really important point. Crushes can become an obsession, if you let them. They start conquering your mind and distract you from your purpose of being in college. Crushes will come and go but your studies and work should be your top priority. Maybe those crushes will turn into boyfriends or girlfriends, but don't let that distract you. No one likes an obsessive person, but we all like someone who is motivated and driven by passion. Focus on your work, and the right person will eventually notice you.

RELATIONSHIP ADVICE

LOVE YOURSELF FIRST

This means that you need to have love for yourself first, because if you don't love yourself, how are you going to love someone else? So, first get to know yourself better and then focus on someone else.

PRIORITIZE

Learn to prioritize things in your life. Don't forget that your first priority is college. If you do get into a relationship, then both of you should have that understanding. You should push each other to do better and achieve your goals. Inspire and encourage each other with work and support in low times. College can be stressful; your relationship can add to the stress but also has the power to relieve you of the stress.

BE INDEPENDENT

Don't lose yourself in a relationship. It is easy to subconsciously take on personality traits of your partner and make them your own. Be an independent individual outside the relationship. It is important that you protect your own personality because being true to who you are will keep you balanced. As an individual, you need to stay true to who you are.

DON'T RUSH

Never rush into something you aren't ready for. Don't do it because people around you are getting into relationships. Before committing to a serious relationship, take baby steps to get to know each other first. However, you should not toy with someone's feelings and emotions. Don't forget about karma because what goes around always comes around.

DON'T TRY TO FIX SOMEONE

In the process of knowing someone, you understand them on a deeper level. There might be aspects about them that you feel are flawed. You must understand that no one is perfect. But that doesn't mean you have to fix the person.

HONESTY AND LOYALTY

Stay honest and loyal to each other. Don't cheat. If you are not interested in them, call it off as soon as you realize it. I had an ex who was dating another girl behind my back. I found out by accident when I saw pictures of her in his phone while making a call. That experience changed me. If you are in the relationship just because you like the idea of having someone around, you're not only lying to yourself but you are also lying to your partner. Be honest while addressing jealousy or insecurities; if you have any, talk it out. Do not let them build up.

MANAGE EXPECTATIONS

Don't expect too much in a relationship, be it with friends, family or your partner. Know what to expect and what not to. At the end of the day, it's no one's responsibility to make you happy. Only you can make yourself happy. No one can fulfill all your expectations.

MENTAL HEALTH

If your relationship makes you cry more than it makes you laugh, it's not healthy. You need to take care of your mental health. You can't let someone control your emotions.

DON'T OVERTHINK

I used to constantly think about my future, about what's going to happen after college, what will happen after two years and so on. The result was me spoiling my present and my relationship. Thinking about the future isn't going to solve anything because you cannot control what comes next, you can only enjoy the present. There will be fears in any relationship. But do not dwell too much upon them.

BE SAFE

Your relationship should make you feel safe. Safe enough to open up emotionally, mentally and physically. It should be a space of mutual understanding and comfort. Also don't let anyone force you in any way.

IT'S OK

It's OK to have your heart broken. It does not mean that your life has come to an end. You'll be OK and that's one thing I can assure you about. There will be nights when you're going to miss them and want to contact them, but remember why it ended. Letting them back into your life may seem like a comfortable choice, but success lies outside your comfort zone.

We all get into fights, either with our partners or friends. Every relationship goes through a rough patch. What matters is how you get out of it together, as one.

FIGHT FOR EACH OTHER

'Is this fight worth it?' We tend to say things in anger that we regret later. Calm down and think about the cause of the fight. If you fight with each other, don't be against each other; instead find a solution together. The only way to get out of a fight is together because if you keep fighting each other, it will tear you apart.

SAY NO TO MIND GAMES

No manipulation and keeping the other person on edge. Don't threaten or blackmail if they go against your wishes. Don't play with your partner's emotions. Don't try to make your partner feel small, insecure or jealous because that isn't healthy. It is emotionally damaging to both of you. Do take respsonibility for your actions. Taking responsibility shows that you value the relationship more than your pride.

KEEP IT PRIVATE

You don't need to involve more people in your fight; it only adds fuel to the fire. Everyone has a different opinion and it will only corrupt yours. You need to sort things out on your own. Don't rely on other people to tell you what to do because in the end, it's your relationship. The opinions of others will not only blind your judgement but also ruin the image of your partner in their eyes.

FIND A SOLUTION

Don't go to sleep without making up after a fight. At the end of the day, both of you are exhausted and tired, and going to sleep feeling upset and angry will only make the pain fester. Make up for the moment, sleep on it and then talk the next day, once both of you have cooled down. Don't bring up past fights; there is a reason the past stays in the past. Do not let your inner negative voice control your mouth.

OH BOY!

Having your ex in your class and facing him every day will require you to be extremely strong. You don't have to be friends with them. Depending on how it ended, your college life will change a bit. You might lose a few old friends and gain a few new ones. Let me tell you about my experience. I broke up with a guy from my class and we had common friends. Those 'friends' became his friends after the break-up, which was weird because they were originally my friends. I didn't know how to go to college and pretend that everything was normal and things had not changed. But what I did learn was that I couldn't stop living my life just because my ex was in the same class. I had to move on. I did feel lonely and my insecurities increased, but I got over it in a few months.

The breakup wasn't the hard part; facing him every day in college was.

You should face your exes like a queen or king. Don't let them see that you're sad or that they have the power to control your emotions. You will get over it. Give yourself time and don't be hard on yourself. If you feel it's difficult to see them in college, that's all right. Concentrate and put all that energy into your work. Once you get used to the break-up, you'll get back to your normal routine.

Don't just remove them from your social media but also delete the photos and mementos too. In my case, those three to four months were the toughest part of my college life. I learnt a lot about myself and the people around me. I saw my ex with other girls on social media and seeing him move on so easily made me realize that he was not worth being sad over. Just do good and be good. That should be your motto.

DON'T FORGET, YOU ARE YOUR FIRST PRIORITY!

THE WORKING LIFE

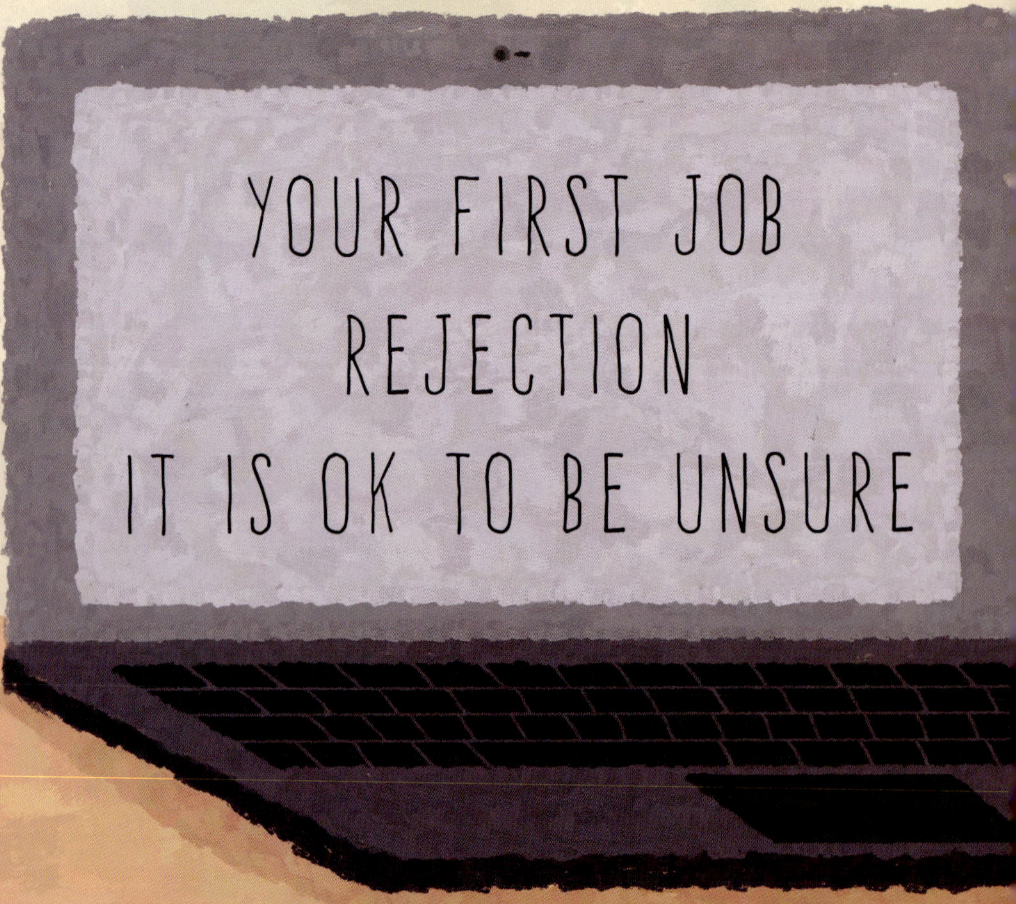

Planner

YOUR FIRST JOB

The best way to make yourself comfortable in a working environment is to do internships during your semester breaks. Internships are a smart way figure out the kind of job you would like to do. You get an understanding of the type of environment you function better in and the kind of firm or studio you wish to work in.

Since internships aren't a long-term commitment, you don't have the stress of being stuck at a place. Even if an internship doesn't work out the way you want it to, you always get to learn from it and make contacts. Here are a few things to keep in mind while stepping into the professional world.

BE CONFIDENT

Dress smart and be confident about your skills and flaws. Keep your head high while taking criticism and compliments, but don't let either of them get to your head. If you don't know something, don't be shy to learn about it. When you start off, you have the chance to learn as much as you can.

SET HEALTHY BOUNDARIES

Know when to say 'no' and when to say 'yes'. As you start off, you might be expected to work overtime or even on weekends. But that is completely up to you. If you aren't OK with working overtime and on weekends, then you should state that at the beginning. Make it clear that you are available only during office hours and not after that.

MIND YOUR BUSINESS

As a new employee, you will be meeting new people. Not everyone is the way they seem to be. You will see their true colours as you interact with them more and more. Do not get involved in office politics and do not let anyone drag you into it. Keep away from people who are two-faced. You will eventually figure out who's good for you and who is toxic.

LEARN

At the workplace, you won't have someone to fall back on like you had in college. Every day will be a new learning experience, not only about your work but also about the people around you. You will learn the professional language, how to deliver work before deadlines, and to express your ideas backed by solid data and research. Also make sure that you are comfortable with PowerPoint, as you will be making a lot of presentations.

STAND UP

If you feel you are being insulted or bullied by someone at work, make sure to inform your manager. But if your manager is the one doing it, make sure to inform HR, in case you cannot approach your boss. It may be that they aren't aware of their behaviour and are doing so unintentionally. Sometimes it is easy to miscommunicate your actions and be unaware of the pain you inflict on the other person.

REJECTION

Doesn't it sting when someone tells us 'NO'? It feels like they can't understand your point of view. But trust me, these 'nos' will shape your life more than all the 'yeses' you get. Every time you get a 'no' in life, be it in college, work, family or relationships, you must learn to pick yourself up and start again.

UNDERSTAND WHY

Be constructive and learn from it. Every time you get a 'no', understand why your idea or proposal was rejected. Do not be defensive. Ask why, get to know your mistakes and how you can fix them for better results next time.

DO NOT GIVE UP

If you feel that your idea is worthy of attention, do not give up on it due to one rejection. Keep working on it. Refine it further and talk to people who are likely to understand it. For example, this book that you are reading was my idea for my graduation project. It was initially rejected, but I did not give up. I believed in my idea and myself.

RESEARCH

If your proposal for a project gets rejected, don't sulk. Talk to the professors or mentors who can help you shape your idea in the right direction. College also helps you get in touch with experts in the industry. Take advantage of that and learn as much as you can. College is the place where you have all the freedom to make mistakes.

STRENGTHENS YOUR SELF-ESTEEM

Rejection at an early age is the best teacher. It builds character and makes you stronger. It makes you less vulnerable when dealing with what others have to say about you. A dear friend of mine always got rejected in college for his ideas, more than any of us collectively. Today, he is more successful in his career than any of us. I'm not saying you can't be successful if you don't get rejected. But what made him who he is today is that he learned how to cope with each rejection and understood not only his audience but also his work in such great depth.

LET IT GO

The best way to move on from rejection is to learn from it. Process what happened and don't let it stop you from progressing. I know it can be a major setback, but it is always for one's own good. Do not let it stop you from creating or learning something new. Just keep moving forward, even if it is only one small step at first.

IT IS OK TO BE UNSURE

'It is OK to be unsure' may not sound very assuring, but it is. You do not need to figure out everything at once. You do not need to plan out everything about the future. Sometimes, the fun lies in not knowing. It makes you look forward to what is next.

When it comes to your career, it is all right to be unsure about what step to take after college. I myself wasn't sure about what I wanted to do. I was insecure about my work and talent, because everyone around me was sure about what they wished to do next, while I was clueless. I was not sure which career path I wanted to take or what job role would suit me best. The only thing I was sure about was that I wanted to be in publishing. That was the only plan I had in my head. After I graduated, my job hunt led to me the graphic-designing position that I am in currently. Alongside, I also found avenues to pursue my interest in book illustrations. I am also interested in Indian folk art, and perhaps at some point in the future, I will pursue it actively. The point is that life is full of surprises, and things always work out for the best in the end.

It is advisable to make a list weighing all the pros and cons of your choices. It makes it easier for you to decide which one to select.

Being unsure isn't always bad; it only means you are open to options and experiences. These experiences will only help you make better judgements and choices in life.

Live each day to the fullest and get as much as experience you can.

Taking baby steps helps in the long run.

Even now, I'm not sure what I want to do next, so I just plan one day at a time. That is my motto and it works very well.

NOTE TO SELF

ABOUT THE AUTHOR

Simran Tapadia is an art enthusiast with a passion for expressionism and realism and enjoys experimenting with different art forms. She started working at the age of seventeen with well-known companies like Jabong, Snapdeal, Lakme and many more. She has created three graphic novels and a colouring book using Indian art styles which she released at Comic Con India 2017 and 2018 as well as a pixel art game at IGX 2017. She is also known for her online comic strip, *The Memesaab.*